SCIENTISTS AT WORK

Secrets of the Deep
MARINE BIOLOGISTS

Mike Unwin

Heinemann
LIBRARY

www.heinemann.co.uk/library

Visit our website to find out more information about Heinemann Library books.

To order:
- ☎ Phone 44 (0) 1865 888066
- 📄 Send a fax to 44 (0) 1865 314091
- 💻 Visit the Heinemann Bookshop at www.heinemann.co.uk/library to browse our catalogue and order online.

First published in Great Britain by Heinemann, Halley Court, Jordan Hill, Oxford, OX2 8EJ, part of Harcourt Education.
Heinemann is a registered trademark of Harcourt Education Ltd.

Editorial: Nancy Dickmann and Joanna Talbot
Design: Richard Parker and Manhattan Design
Illustrations: Darren Lingard
Picture Research: Mica Brancic and Virginia Stroud-Lewis
Production: Alison Parsons

Originated by Modern Age
Printed and bound in China by Leo Paper Group

13 digit ISBN 978 0431 14928 8
12 11 10 09 08
10 9 8 7 6 5 4 3 2 1

British Library Cataloguing in Publication Data
Unwin, Mike
Secrets of the deep : marine biologists. - (Scientists at work)
1. Marine biologists - Juvenile literature 2. Marine biology - Juvenile literature
I. Title
578.7'7'023

A full catalogue record for this book is available from the British Library.

Acknowledgements
The Publishers would like to thank the following for permission to reproduce photographs: ©Alamy pp. **15** (Jeff Rotman); ©Corbis pp. **5** (Louie Psihoyos) **7** (Jeffrey L. Rotman), **11**, **27** (Stephen Frink), **17** (Jonathan Blair), **19**, **22** (Jacques Pavlovsky/Sygma), **26** (Sergio Pitamitz); ©Getty Images pp. **8** (Heinrich van den Berg), **20** (The Image Bank/Frans Lemmens), **18** (Taxi/Chris Howes); ©Marine Quest p. **25**; ©Nature Picture Library pp. **10** (Tony Heald), **14** (Peter Scoones); ©NHPA p. **16**; ©PhotoLibrary.com pp. **9** (Animals Animals/Earth Scenes/Franklin Viola), **13** (Pacific Stock/Fleetham Drive), **21** (StockByte), **24** (Alaska Stock Images/ Manewal Ernest); ©Science Photo Library pp. **4** (Peter Scoones), **6** (Pascal Goetcheluck), **12** (Eye of Science), **23** (NASA).

Cover photograph of scuba diver reproduced with permission of Science Photo Library/Alexis Rosenfeld.

The publishers would like to thank Virginia H. Garrison for her assistance in the preparation of this book.

Every effort has been made to contact copyright holders of any material reproduced in this book. Any omissions will be rectified in subsequent printings if notice is given to the publishers.

Disclaimer
All the Internet addresses (URLs) given in this book were valid at the time of going to press. However, due to the dynamic nature of the Internet, some addresses may have changed, or sites may have changed or ceased to exist since publication. While the author and Publishers regret any inconvenience this may cause readers, no responsibility for any such changes can be accepted by either the author or the Publishers.

Contents

Any words appearing in the text in bold, **like this**, are explained in the Glossary.

What do marine biologists do?

Life on Earth began in the oceans more than 3.5 billion years ago. That's 2.5 billion years before it began on land. Things that live in the ocean are called marine **organisms**, and marine biologists are the scientists who study them.

The oceans cover 71% of the Earth's surface, and there are many more organisms living in the sea than on land. They vary in size from microscopic bacteria to enormous whales. Marine biologists study how and where they all live.

Marine organisms provide us with food and other important **resources**. They also help keep life going on land by producing **oxygen**, which plants and animals need to live. Marine biologists teach us how marine organisms live and how we can protect them.

The coelacanth is a fish from prehistoric times. Marine biologists only re-discovered it in 1938.

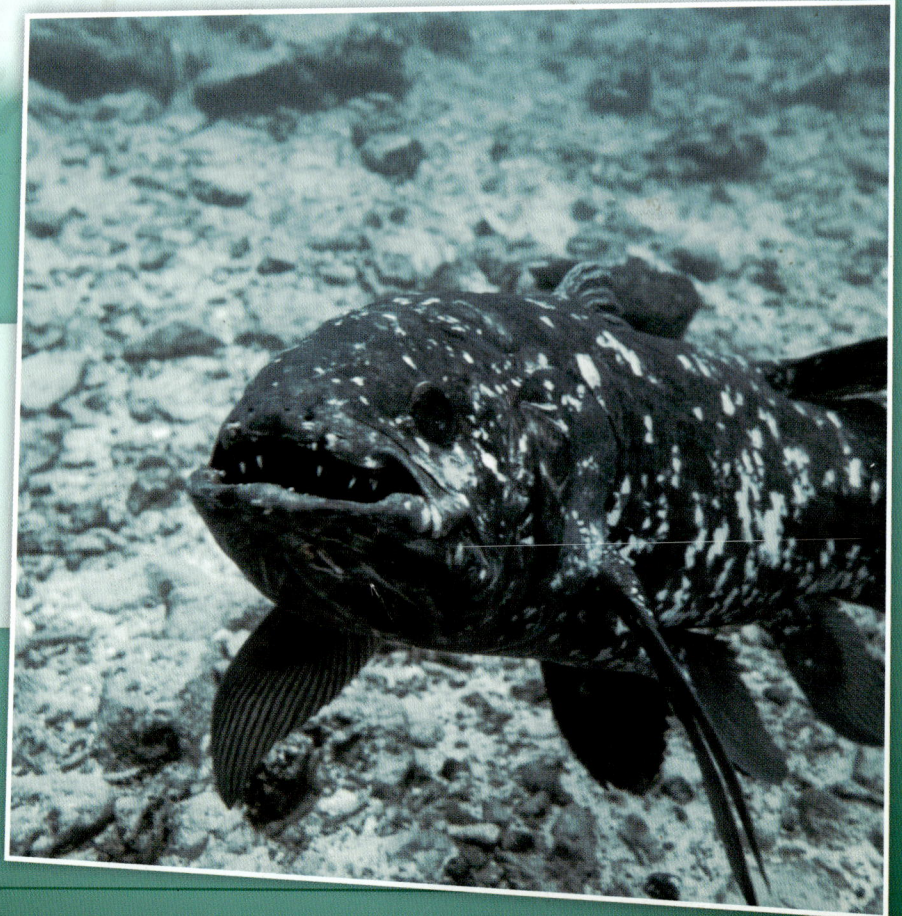

The history of marine biology

The modern science of marine biology became popular in Europe during the 1800s, when explorers started making new discoveries in distant oceans.

By the 1870s, the first laboratories for studying marine life had been built. During the early 1900s, new diving machines allowed marine biologists to study life deep in the ocean for the first time. Technology continues to develop and helps us to keep learning more. There is still much more to discover – scientists believe that 81% of the oceans haven't been explored yet.

Some marine biologists study whale sharks, the biggest fish on Earth.

WHO'S WHO: Jacques-Yves Cousteau

Jacques-Yves Cousteau was one of the world's most famous marine biologists. He introduced the undersea world to millions through films and TV series. He also helped invent the **aqualung**, a tank of air worn by divers to help them breathe underwater, which made scuba diving possible. Later in his life Cousteau became a **conservationist** campaigning to protect the oceans. He died in 1997.

Different jobs?

Marine biologists do many different jobs. Some travel to exciting places such as tropical reefs or frozen ice caps. Others stay closer to home, perhaps working by the seashore where they live.

Out and about

Marine biologists spend much of their time working on or by the sea. This is called "fieldwork". It allows them to observe marine organisms in their natural environment. For instance, one marine biologist might work on board a ship collecting young fish. Another might dig up **estuary** mud to see what kind of marine organisms it contains.

Some marine biologists work underwater. This way they can observe marine creatures behaving naturally. It also gives them the opportunity to write down observations and take photographs.

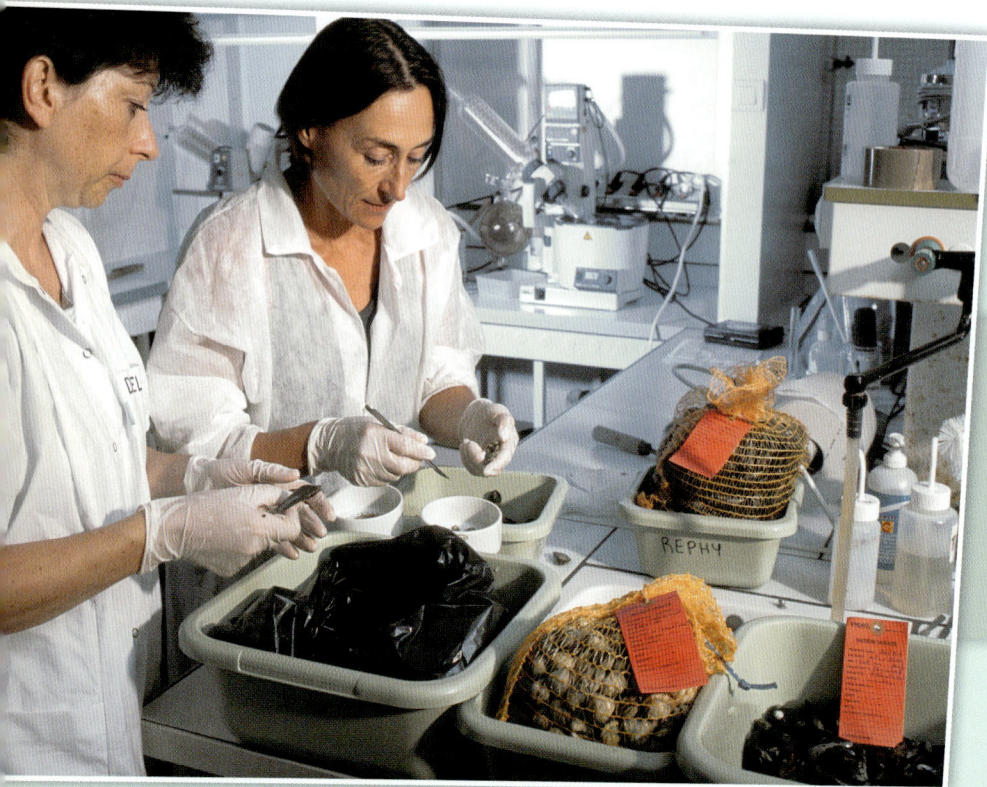

Marine biologists often take marine organisms back to the laboratory to study them.

Marine biologists work for up to ten days at a time in the *Aquarius* underwater habitat.

In the lab

Back in the **laboratory**, marine biologists study the information and samples they have collected from "the field". They use **microscopes** and special equipment to help them. These tell them important things, such as how many kinds of organism there are, what they eat, and whether their environment is changing.

Marine biologists also do a lot of work on computers. Those studying fish populations, for instance, use special computer programs to analyse their **data**. This helps them predict fish populations of the future.

TOOLS OF THE TRADE: UNDERWATER HABITATS

Underwater habitats are structures built on the sea floor where marine biologists, called "aquanauts", live and work. They are supplied with air, food, and water, and have special scientific equipment. *Aquarius* is an underwater habitat off the coast of the Florida Keys, USA. Marine biologists can stay here while they study the nearby coral reef.

Where do marine biologists work?

The ocean consists of many different places where things live, called habitats. Each habitat has its own community of marine organisms. Marine biologists study every habitat to find out what lives there and how to keep it healthy.

Male fiddler crabs, which live in mangrove forests, use their one enormous claw to signal to females.

Shorelines

Coastal habitats support lots of marine life, from starfish in rock pools to worms in the sand. Each has to cope with conditions that change daily as the **tide** goes in and out. Seabirds also find food and shelter along the shore.

Mangrove trees grow along tropical coasts. Their roots are able to grow in the shallow, salty water. The water in mangrove forests is home to unique animals, such as fiddler crabs.

Undersea forests

Seaweeds are **algae** that grow in the sea. The largest type is kelp, which prefers cold seas. It forms underwater "forests", anchored on the seabed with the tops floating at the surface about 30 metres (98 feet) above. Sea otters are among many creatures that live there.

Coral reefs

Coral reefs are only found in warm, tropical waters. Although they look like gardens of colourful plants, they are formed of **limestone** laid down by tiny animals called polyps. Reefs support a huge variety of marine organisms and also protect coastlines from storms. Some last thousands of years.

Marine biologists can observe a rich variety of life on coral reefs.

TRICKS OF THE TRADE: NIGHT DIVING

Marine biologists dive at night, using torches, to study animal behaviour that only happens after dark. For instance, many reef fish hide away in narrow cracks at night and change their colour so that **predators** cannot spot them. Night time is also when most reef fish lay their eggs. They swim up and release their eggs into the **current**, which carries them away to new homes.

Out at sea

Marine organisms spread out more in the open ocean than in coastal regions. Although the sea may look the same at the surface, currents concentrate food in particular areas. Small fish such as sardines feed on gatherings of **plankton**. Larger fish, such as tuna, travel widely in search of sardines.

Some animals, such as whales and sea turtles, make long journeys to feed and have their young. Marine biologists study them to find out where they go. They mark some with **satellite tags**. These give off electronic signals that help to track how they move.

Large fish such as great white sharks hunt smaller fish in the ocean.

Frozen waters

In **polar regions** the sea surface freezes during winter to form huge ice sheets. Marine biologists have found that algae grow on the bottom of the ice and provide food for shrimp-like creatures called krill. Larger animals such as penguins and whales feed on the krill.

Deep down

The bottom of the ocean is 11 kilometres (6.8 miles) deep in some places – deeper than Mount Everest is high. This is a hard habitat to explore because a diver cannot usually dive down below 100 metres (328 feet). The water is very cold and dark, since no sunlight reaches it. The weight of water pressing down also creates enormous **water pressure**.

Marine biologists explore the seabed in machines called deep-sea submersibles. They have discovered some amazing things about the creatures that live there. For example, some creatures produce a special chemical light, called bioluminescence, for communicating in the dark.

ROVs use video cameras to film what they find, and mechanical tools to take specimens and measurements.

TOOLS OF THE TRADE: ROVs

In places where marine biologists cannot reach, they sometimes use an ROV. This stands for remotely operated vehicle. It is a submarine robot that sends information back along cables to the researcher.

What do marine biologists study?

Marine biologists study marine organisms that range in size from tiny bacteria to enormous whales. They also study how the oceans and their organisms are affected by humans.

Plankton

The ocean's biomass is the total weight of all its living things. Over 98% of the ocean's biomass consists of tiny floating organisms called plankton. Most are phytoplankton – microscopic plants that drift near the surface. The rest are zooplankton, which are tiny animals that eat phytoplankton.

Marine biologists use special equipment to study plankton. These include remote-controlled nets that capture samples deep down in the ocean. By working out the amount of plankton, they can predict the populations of other animals, such as fish, that depend on it for food.

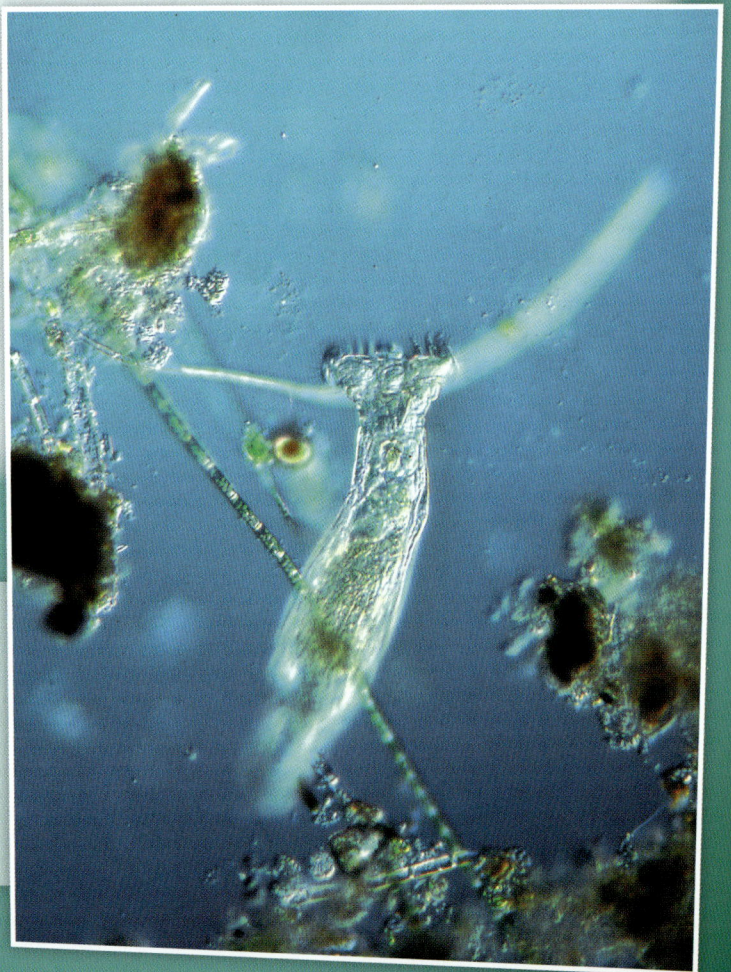

Microscopes can show plankton (shown here) hundreds or thousands of times larger than in real life, so that you can see what they look like.

Invertebrates

Invertebrates are animals without backbones, such as insects, worms, and snails. Among the simplest are sponges, which filter their food from the water. Other types include molluscs (invertebrates with shells, such as clams) and crustaceans (invertebrates with segmented bodies, such as crabs).

Marine biologists have discovered that some invertebrates have special relationships with fish. For instance, stinging sea anemones allow clownfish to shelter among their tentacles. The fish help protect the anemones from their enemies. In return, the anemone offers the fish a hiding place from predators.

The clownfish does not feel the stinging tentacles of anemones.

The science behind it: Marine food chains

Marine organisms are linked to each other by what they eat. This is called a food chain. Phytoplankton are the first link in each food chain since they make their own food from sunlight. This means they are "producers". Zooplankton eat phytoplankton, so they are called "consumers". Animals that eat zooplankton, such as fish, are called "secondary consumers". Each habitat has many food chains linked together in a "food web" (see pages 28–29).

The leafy seadragon looks a bit like seaweed. This is to provide a disguise and help it hide from predators.

Fish

About 20,000 **species** of fish live in the sea. They range from tiny seahorses to enormous whale sharks, which are up to 12 metres (39 feet) long. Fish provide food and work for millions of people, so marine biologists study them closely.

Fish have many special features for living underwater, including **gills**, which they use for breathing. Fish fall into two main groups. Most have a skeleton made out of bones, so are called "bony fish". The other main group has skeletons made of more flexible material, called **cartilage**. Sharks and rays are in this group.

Some fish can do weird and wonderful things. Puffer fish inflate themselves with water so that nothing can swallow them. Anglerfish tempt their prey closer by wiggling a long spine above their head like a fishing rod. Flying fish even leap out of the water and glide through the air to escape danger.

Understanding sharks

Scary movies make us believe that sharks are blood-thirsty killers. But marine biologists have shown that this is not true. Of 370 species of shark, only four are generally a threat to humans. And attacks happen very rarely – sharks normally avoid or ignore people. Marine biologists have found that sharks have some amazing abilities. For instance, they are very sensitive to electricity and can even use electricity in ocean currents to help them find their way.

TOOLS OF THE TRADE: SHARK CAGE

Scientists who study sharks sometimes enter the water in a metal cage for protection. This means they can closely observe the sharks in safety. Most shark species are safe to approach without a cage. Experienced divers can tell how a shark is going to behave and will move away if it looks aggressive or unhappy.

A cage offers a safe way for divers to get close to sharks when they are feeding.

Whales, dolphins, and other marine mammals

Whales and dolphins, known to scientists as cetaceans, are mammals. This means that they are **warm-blooded**, give birth to live young, and **suckle** their babies on milk.

Cetaceans are well adapted to life in the ocean. Instead of legs, they have flippers and a tail to power them along. Like all mammals, they breathe air into their lungs. They breathe through a **blowhole** which is a nostril on top of their heads. With water to support their weight, some have grown enormous. The blue whale can reach 100 tonnes (100,000 kilograms) and is the largest animal that has ever lived.

There are two kinds of cetacean. Toothed whales, which include dolphins, have teeth for catching fish. Baleen whales, which include the blue whale, have sieve-like plates called baleen in their mouth that filter plankton from the water.

Humpback whales can leap right out of the water. This is known as breaching. The splash can be heard from over a mile (1.6 km) away.

Some cetaceans have their own language. Male humpback whales, for instance, sing to attract females. Marine biologists listen to their songs underwater using devices called hydrophones. They have learned that each male has its own personal tune.

Seals

Seals and sea lions are marine mammals that have descended from a bear-like land ancestor. Unlike cetaceans, they still have fur and nostrils, and come ashore to give birth. There are many kinds of seal, including the fierce leopard seals that hunt penguins, and walruses that dig up shellfish with their tusks.

Putting a satellite tag on this dolphin will help marine biologists to track its progress.

The science behind it: Echolocation

Dolphins can catch fish underwater using a technique called echolocation, which is also how bats catch insects in flight. They make high-pitched clicking and whistling sounds that bounce back off fish. This shows the dolphin exactly where the fish are, even when it is too dark to see.

Why are the oceans so important?

The oceans provide us with many precious resources. Marine biologists work to ensure that we use these without damaging the marine environment.

In the air

The oceans' most important gift to us is in the air we breathe. Phytoplankton produce 90% of the Earth's oxygen. Without oxygen no animal could live on Earth.

Phytoplankton also absorb a gas called carbon dioxide (CO_2) from the atmosphere. All animals produce CO_2 by breathing, but people also generate it by burning **fossil fuels** for energy. Too much CO_2 in the atmosphere helps cause **global warming**, so by absorbing CO_2 the ocean helps protect the Earth's climate.

However, marine biologists have discovered that too much CO_2 dissolved in the oceans damages marine organisms. For example, it can prevent snails from growing shells.

The oceans help absorb carbon dioxide that enters the atmosphere when we burn fossil fuels.

Tourists visit tropical reefs to enjoy the marine life for themselves.

The climate

The oceans also help control the Earth's climate. They store lots of energy in the form of heat, then transport it around the world in currents. This cools tropical seas and warms cooler ones, which also affects temperatures on land. It is another way in which oceans help reduce global warming.

Getting around

We once used ships to explore the globe. Now they are still the best way to transport heavy cargo around the world. Marine biologists study how shipping affects marine life, especially by its waste (such as spilled oil) and noise.

Having fun

The sea also provides enjoyment. Millions of people head for the coast to relax, have fun, and enjoy the marine life. Tourism developments, such as hotels or harbours, can damage fragile habitats and disturb marine life. But tourism also gives us a good reason to look after marine habitats.

The oceans' resources

Many people depend on what they can take from the oceans. This includes food such as fish, and raw materials such as oil.

Fishing changes

Fishing has changed over time. Local fishermen in **developing countries** may still cast a homemade net from a small boat. But elsewhere fleets of huge boats catch thousands of tonnes of fish each day.

Fish farms offer an alternative to fishing in the sea. The fish are raised in special floating enclosures instead of being caught from the oceans. However, fish farms can spread disease, pollute the marine environment, and damage coastal habitats, such as mangroves.

Marine biologists work with the fishing industry to check on the numbers of fish and study things that affect them, such as their food supplies. They study how people catch fish and help design nets that are safer for other marine life. They also help fish farmers find ways to reduce damage to the marine environment.

Fishing is one of many ways people can make a living from the sea.

Marine biologists help look after seabirds that are damaged by oil spills.

Digging deep

People use special machinery to dig deep into the ocean floor. Some extract sand or gravel to use in building. Others search for valuable minerals, such as manganese. Huge drills also pump oil and gas from the seabed, to supply energy for our homes and industries. But mining and drilling can destroy marine habitats, while clouds of waste can harm the growth of plankton by blocking out sunlight.

WHO'S WHO: Sylvia Earle

Sylvia Earle is a famous American marine biologist. She led the first ever team of women aquanauts and holds the world record for the deepest solo dive. She is also an expert on oil spills. Earle has led research trips to famous spill sites to discover what damage has been done and how we can help the environment to recover.

Why are the oceans in danger?

People once thought the oceans were so big that we could never harm them. Now scientists know that what we do has a huge effect. Because of us, many marine creatures and habitats are now at risk.

Taking too much

To feed our growing population, we are taking too many fish from the sea. Populations of some fish, including cod and tuna, are falling faster than they can recover. In some places fishermen have no fish left to catch.

Harming habitats

We are damaging marine habitats all around the world. We are poisoning coral reefs, building on beaches where turtles nest, and clearing mangroves for shrimp farms.

We are also dumping waste, such as **industrial waste**, oil, and nuclear waste into the ocean. **Fertilisers**, **sewage**, and other pollutants seep down rivers into the sea, leaving some coasts so polluted that nothing can live there.

Too much fishing causes fish populations to fall fast.

Going, going, gone

Today there are more than 1,200 **endangered** marine species, including many whales, turtles, and sharks. They are in danger from pollution and shrinking food supplies.

Climate change

The worst threat to the sea may now be global warming. Warmer seas melt ice sheets, kill coral, and cause more hurricanes. High sea levels, caused by melting ice, bring coastal flooding. Ocean changes can seriously affect weather conditions on land.

The green patches on this satellite image show how algal blooms in the Caspian Sea are visible from space.

TOOLS OF THE TRADE: SATELLITES

Marine biologists use satellite images to spot problems at sea. Pollution can cause rapid growths of algae, called "algal blooms". These can spread over huge areas and their red or green colour is visible from space. They use up so much oxygen that other marine organisms die.

Marine biologists helping out

Marine biologists do more than just study the oceans. They also help us look after them. This work is called marine conservation biology. Marine biologists find out where there are problems in the ocean. One important thing they study is **sustainability**. This means working out how we can use the ocean's resources without using them all up. "Sustainable" fishing, for example, is fishing that protects fish populations.

Marine biologists helped governments make the Southern Ocean a sanctuary for animals such as these Adelie penguins.

Being heard

Marine biologists publish their work so that we can all learn more about the oceans. They also give advice on how to manage ocean resources. Some work for conservation groups, who encourage governments to make decisions that protect the oceans.

More to learn

Marine biologists keep discovering more about the sea. For instance, in 1998 they discovered the mimic octopus. This amazing animal can impersonate dangerous sea snakes, stingrays, and scorpion fish by changing colour and moving in different ways. These clever disguises help keep its enemies away.

The mimic octopus lives in the sea around Indonesia.

Ocean cures

Marine organisms can also bring us medicine. Blood from horseshoe crabs, for example, contains chemicals that help doctors check whether drugs are safe for their patients. Scientists believe that the sea may provide many more medicines in the future. They are conducting research to see how marine organisms can help in the fight against cancer.

WHO'S WHO: Rachel Carson

Rachel Carson was an American marine biologist who played a big part in founding today's environmental movement. She is best known for her book *Silent Spring*, which warned about the dangers of pollution, both at sea and on the land. Carson died in 1964. Today the Rachel Carson prize is given to women who have made a major contribution to conservation.

What does it take to be a marine biologist?

So you want to be a marine biologist? Great! The world needs more marine biologists. But it won't be easy. It will take hard work, skill, and dedication.

Find out more

First, find out as much as you can about marine life. Look in books, at websites, or on TV. Explore the seaside whenever you can. What marine organisms can you find along the shore? Take notes, pictures, or sketches, then look up what you saw later. If you live far from the sea, you could visit an aquarium.

Study

You will need to study hard at school, especially in science and maths. Marine biologists need to understand these subjects. Most go to college after leaving school to study marine biology or another science subject.

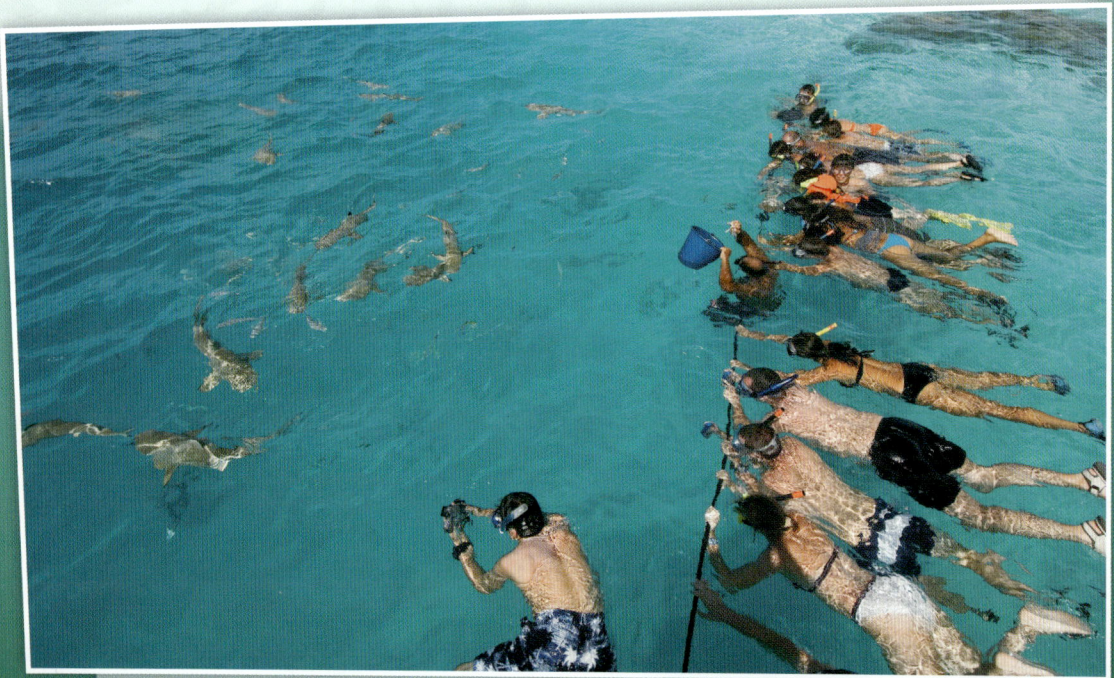

Explore coastal habitats whenever you get the chance.

TOOLS OF THE TRADE: SCUBA

Scuba stands for Self-Contained Underwater Breathing Apparatus. It consists of a tank of air on a diver's back that connects to their mouth by a tube, so they can breathe underwater. The mouthpiece has a device called a regulator, which helps the diver breathe in and out easily. Scuba diving is a special skill that takes training and practice.

Marine biologists need special skills, such as scuba diving.

Starting out

Some students work as volunteers after they leave school, often before joining college. They may do marine conservation work at home or perhaps join an exciting expedition abroad. Volunteering can give you valuable experience and important skills, such as scuba diving or using computer programs.

Different jobs

If you do become a marine biologist, you must decide what interests you most. No marine biologist can study everything. There are many different jobs. For example, icthyologists study fish, phycologists study algae, and mammologists study marine mammals.

Marine food webs

A food web is a complicated network of food chains. All marine food webs contain phytoplankton, because these are the first link in every marine food chain. They also all contain zooplankton, which feed directly on phytoplankton. In a food web many animals eat more than one thing. Here is an example of a marine food web. This one is in the Antarctic.

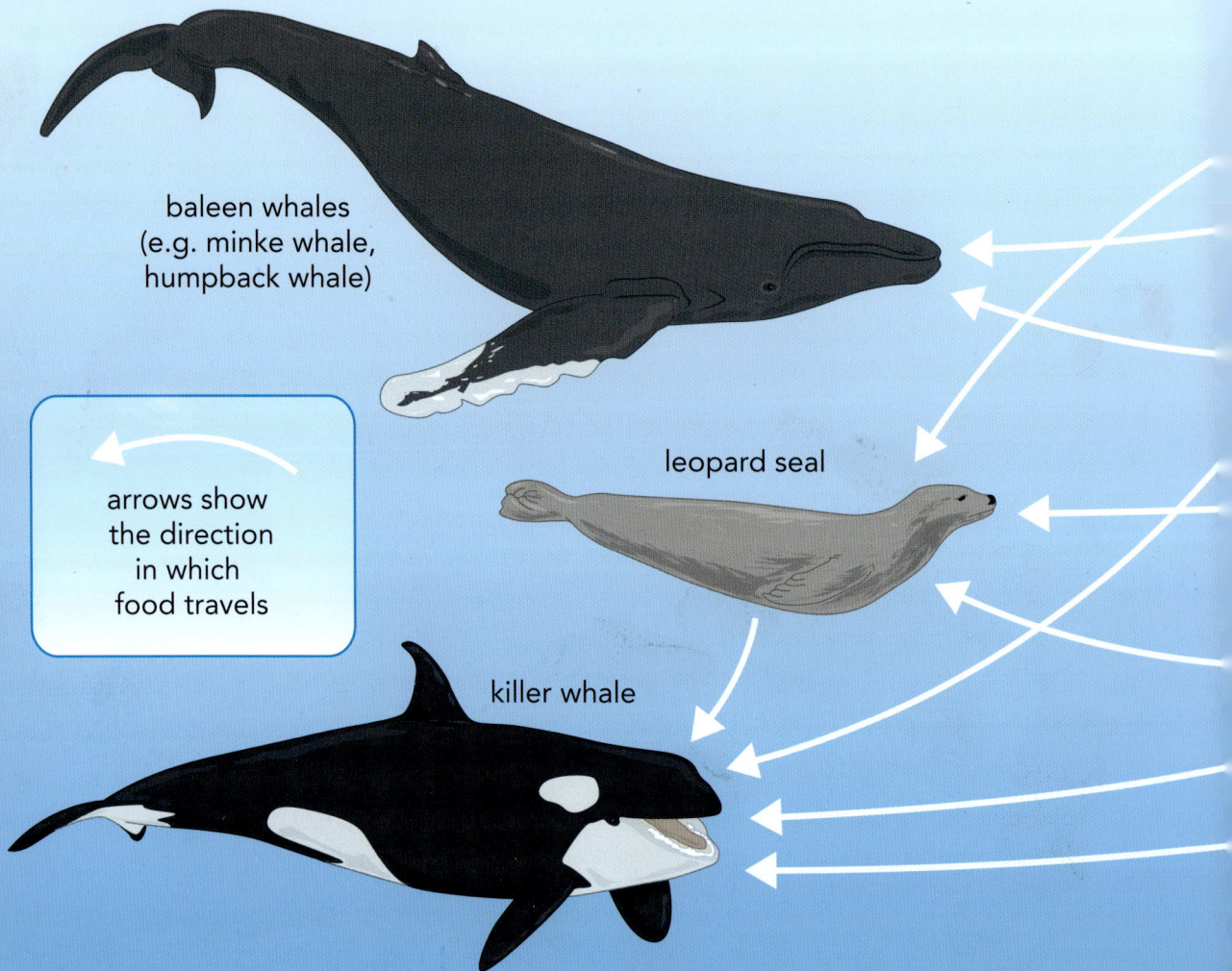

baleen whales
(e.g. minke whale,
humpback whale)

arrows show
the direction
in which
food travels

leopard seal

killer whale

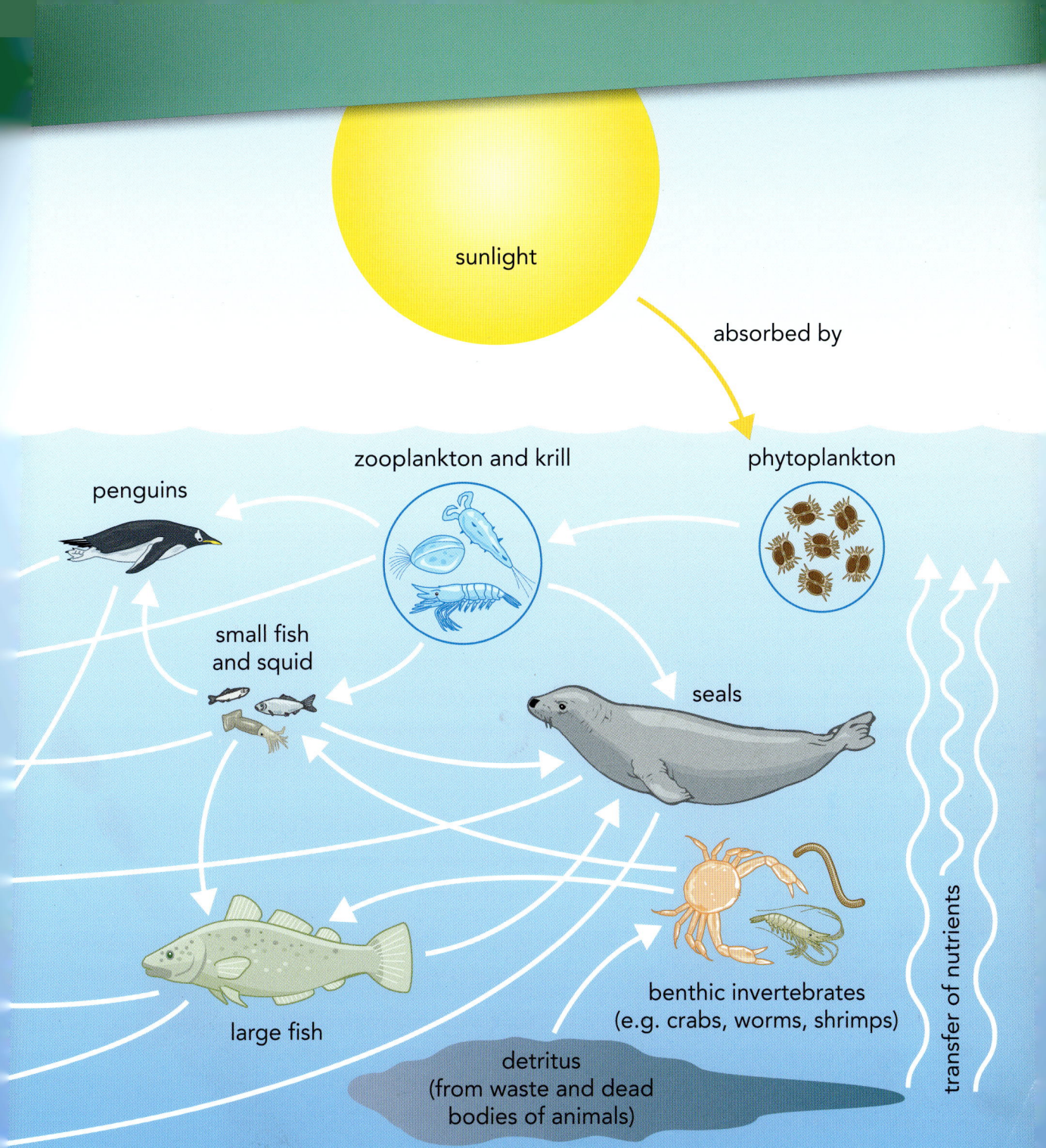

sunlight

absorbed by

zooplankton and krill

phytoplankton

penguins

small fish and squid

seals

transfer of nutrients

large fish

benthic invertebrates
(e.g. crabs, worms, shrimps)

detritus
(from waste and dead
bodies of animals)

Every food web also contains detritus, which is waste material from dead animals and plants – including their dead bodies. Detritus in turn is food for scavengers. They break it down into minerals and nutrients, which re-enter the food web and help phytoplankton to make more food from sunlight.

Glossary

algae simple water plants with no stems or flowers

aqualung tank of air worn by divers for breathing underwater

blowhole nostril of a whale, on top of its head

cartilage stretchy body tissue between some bones and in the nose and ears

conservationist person who works to protect living creatures and their habitats

current movement of water in a river or the ocean

data information collected by scientists

developing country poor nation, where most people rely upon farming for a living

endangered in danger of dying out

estuary wide mouth of a river

fertilizer product used to make plants and crops grow better

fossil fuel fuel, such as oil or coal, formed from ancient deposits of fossilised plants

gills openings at each side of a fish's body which allow it to breathe

global warming planet Earth becoming warmer due to climate change

industrial waste waste material created by factories and other industrial activities

laboratory place with special equipment where scientists conduct research

limestone type of rock formed from the bodies of tiny marine organisms

microscope scientific instrument that magnifies tiny things allowing them to be seen

organism living thing, such as a plant or animal

oxygen gas in the atmosphere that plants produce and animals breathe

plankton tiny plants and animals that float in the sea

polar regions areas that surround the north and south poles

predator animal that hunts and eats other animals

resource something that people use

satellite tag marker attached to an animal that transmits signals from a satellite

sewage human waste piped from homes and buildings

species single, unique kind of living thing

suckle drink milk from mother

sustainability ability to be used again and again without risk of running out

tide regular rise and fall of the level of the sea

warm-blooded having a constantly warm body temperature. Mammals are warm-blooded; fish are not.

water pressure the force against a surface caused by water pressing on it

Find out more

Further reading

Amazing Journeys: To the Depths of the Ocean, Rod Theodorou
(Heinemann Library, 2006)

Awesome Oceans, Michael Bright (Aladdin, 2002). A series of books about the oceans
and marine life. Titles include *Amazing Animal Journeys*, *Animals of the Icy Seas*,
Animals of the Tropical Seas, and *People and the Sea*.

Earth Files: Oceans, Anita Ganeri (Heinemann Library, 2002)

First Encyclopedia Of Seas And Oceans by Ben Denne (Usborne, 2001)

Habitat Explorer: Ocean Explorer, Greg Pyers (Raintree, 2004)

Mapping Earthforms: Oceans and Seas, Catherine Chambers and Nicholas Lapthorn
(Heinemann Library, 2007)

Our World: Oceans, Katie Harker (Hodder Wayland, 2005)

The Sea: Exploring Life on an Ocean Planet, Robert Burleigh and Philip Plisson
(Abrams, 2003)

Websites

www.marinebio.com
Everything you want to know about marine biology, sea creatures, and the oceans,
with a strong focus on conservation. For older readers.

www.bbc.co.uk/nature/blueplanet
Find out about the natural history of the world's oceans and ocean life.

www.mbgnet.net
Information about ocean ecosystems, distinguishing temperate and tropical oceans.
Click on the "animals" tab to find information about ocean life. This site also has lots of
useful links.

Index